Acknowle

Acknowledgement is ma   ɯe generosity of the
following sponsors:

A.F. (Budge) Adams
Dover Harbour Board
Eurotunnel
George Hammond (shipping) Ltd
National Westminster Bank PLC
Pfizer Ltd
David Shaw M.P.
Jack Woolford

Acknowledgement also to Dover Museum and
A.F. Adams for providing many of the photographs
and illustrations. ©

DOVER

DOVER'S HIDDEN FORTRESS

The history and preservation of the Western Heights fortifications

JOHN PEVERLEY

The
White Cliffs Countryside Project on the Western Heights

KIRK ALEXANDER

Contents

Introduction

THE OBJECTIVES OF THE DOVER SOCIETY WHICH WAS FOUNDED IN 1988 are to promote high standards of planning and architecture, to interest and inform the public in the geography, history, archæology, natural history and architecture of the town and to secure the preservation, protection, development and improvement of features of historical and public interest.

We now take for granted the desire to conserve our heritage and environment but thirty years ago it was possible for the magnificent Napoleonic fortifications on Dover's Western Heights to be regarded by an otherwise responsible Borough Council as a suitable dumping ground for domestic rubbish and as a potential site for industrial development.

Conservation was then very much a minority concern and it was remarkable indeed that rescue of these fortifications should have been conceived and promoted by a locally-born architect, John Peverley, then working three thousand miles away in the United States.

Thirty years later the *Dover Society*, itself wholly committed to the conservation and preservation of this ancient monument, invited John Peverley to address the 1991 AGM of the Society on "The Fortifications, their Destruction, Restoration and Preservation 1959 – 1990". Following his talk to the Society the idea of this publication was conceived.

John Peverley had also produced an earlier article entitled "The Brick Cliffs of Dover" for publication in the Architectural Review in 1959. The Society is grateful that he has agreed to the inclusion of both these works in this booklet.

To complement this comprehensive work and to extend the visitor's knowledge and enjoyment of this important site, the Society felt that this book should be extended to include the work of the White Cliffs Countryside Project on the Western Heights including details of their guided walks

Jack Woolford, Chairman, Dover Society

Glossary

Bastion: A projecting work at the angle or in the line of a fortification, to bring flanking fire on an assailant.

Batter: A term used to describe the slope of a wall upwards from ground level.

Caponnière: A passage or bastion projecting from the main wall of a redoubt or citadel into the surrounding ditch; developed by Albert Dürer, to bring flanking fire on an assailant.

Casemate: A bomb-proof vault in a fortress, housing some of the garrison or guns, and constructed to form part of the walls facing into a ditch.

Citadel: A stronghold or fortress used as a storehouse and centre of a defensive organisation, and as a refuge for final retreat.

Embrasure: The opening in a wall through which guns may be fired, usually with bevelled sides to provide a wide angle of fire.

Fosse: A ditch around a fortification, usually filled with water.

Glacis: An open plain in front of a fortification where assailants would be open to fire.

Line: A deep ditch or moat.

Ravelin: A detached work with a parapet and ditch, forming a salient angle in front of the main fortification.

Redoubt: A detached outwork of great strength, able to fire in any direction, without re-entrant angles and without flanking defences.

Terreplein: The upper surface of a rampart where guns are mounted.

Traverses and parallels: The traverse is a zig-zag trench used by assailants for approaching a besieged fortress so that fire could not be directed down its length: a series of 'parallel" trenches were constructed parallel to the fortification as the traverse trench proceeded, to accommodate guards for the excavators of the traverse. This method of attack was introduced by Vauban in 1673.

Aerial view of the Western Outworks and Citadel

Access to the Western Heights

Entering Dover from the west, one sees only a scrub-covered, steep-sided hill rising up behind the houses with a hint of modern rooftops and fencing on the plateau summit. Approaching from the east, however, or standing in the town, one has a very different perception. This is not the usual chalk ridge, but a hill cut away into an intriguing series of man-made terraces and slopes, half hiding a variety of features which just ask to be explored.

Access is easy by the route sign-posted from the first A20 roundabout on the outskirts of Dover. Follow the winding South Military Road, under the trees and up to the car park/viewing platform on the right, or drive up to it from Dover via the North Military Road. Easy paths lead to the St. Martin's Battery, the top of the Grand Shaft and the grass-covered Drop Redoubt, and superb views over the port and the Channel – including the French coast on a clear day – are a bonus. Access is also provided by Drop Redoubt Road.

1

Energetic walkers following the North Downs Way or parking in Adrian Street can approach via the Sixty-four Steps at Cowgate and even steeper chalk steps above, to be rewarded with a sudden close-up of part of the Drop Redoubt and its massive brick-lined surrounding "line". A footpath along the floor of the line is accessible to the agile and adventurous. Others can continue along the safely fenced hillside path beside another dry moat and down a steep, orchid-covered bank into the military road. A signpost directs one to the so-called Knights Templar's Church, beyond which a track leads to a grassy platform below the imposing façade of the Citadel Officers Mess (not open to the public).

The northern bastions can be reached by a long footpath round the ramparts while the slopes below can be traversed at several levels.

Every view from a vantage point is a gem and any friendly cattle encountered are harmless and a vital part of the grazing plan to encourage wild flowers and butterflies. Strong shoes are essential. The chalk can be slippery in wet weather. Happy exploring!

May Jones–Dover Society

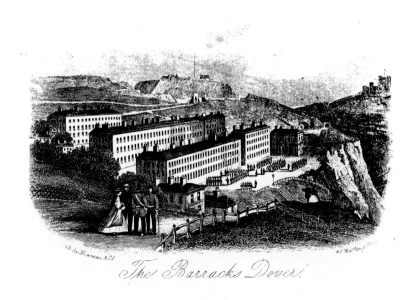

The Barracks Dover!

The BRICK CLIFFS of DOVER:

The Fortifications on the Western Heights

An edited version of an article by
JOHN PEVERLEY
published in
The Architectural Review in 1959

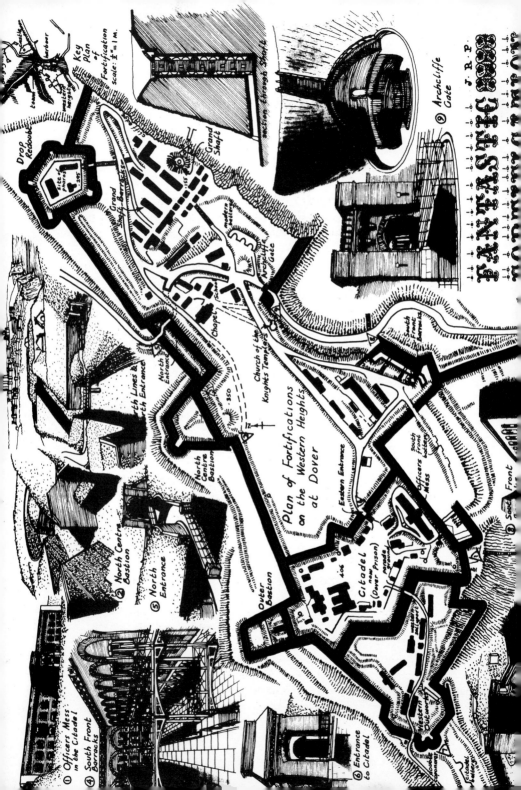

FANTASTIC

FORTRESS

J. R. P.

Plan of Fortifications
on the Western Heights
at Dover

Key plan
of Fortification
scale: ¼ = 1 m.

Section through Shaft

Drop
Redoubt

Grand Shaft

Grand Shaft Barracks

Site of Old 355

155

Chapel

Church of the Knights Templars

350

North Centre Bastion

North Lines & North Entrance

Archcliffe Gate

Outer Bastion

Eastern Entrance

Citadel
now
(Dover Prison)

Entrance to Citadel

South Front Subway

Officers Mess

South Front Barracks

40

① Officers Mess in the Citadel
④ South Front Barracks
② North Centre Bastion
⑤ North Entrance
⑥ Entrance to Citadel
⑦ South Front
⑧ Archcliffe Gate

The Fortifications on the Western Heights

UNKNOWN TO MOST PEOPLE, there exists on the hills to the west of the town and port of Dover a fortification which was considered at the beginning of this century to be the strongest and most elaborate in the country. Although the development of this fortification has continued sporadically since Roman times, being strongly influenced by the invention of gun powder in 1320, the introduction and development of artillery, and a succession of wars, the most intense period of military construction in Dover occurred in the twelfth, thirteenth and nineteenth centuries.

The nineteenth century fortifications which occupy the hills on the Western Heights are of great interest and historical importance as an example of a most ingenious type of defence.

The hill was first fortified in 1779 during the war with America, France, Spain and Holland but the defences provided then were only in the form of earthworks and cannon. Nothing further was constructed until the war with France of 1793, following the French Revolution. Napoleon was threatening to invade and a plan was drawn up to make the Western Heights the largest and strongest fortification in the country, large enough to house a major section of British Army in hiding, for whilst the fortification was never expected to be directly attacked from the sea, it was intended to be used as a base for attacking the rear of Napoleon's army after it had effected a landing, presumably somewhere between Hythe and Rye.

Because of this curious stratagem the colossal expenditure incurred in the construction of these fortifications was not readily accepted by those with intelligence. William Cobbett, who had some knowledge of military fortifications, having made a report of those in Canada, says in his "Rural Rides" that when he visited the Western Heights in 1823 a 'couple of square miles or more were hollowed out like a honeycomb … that either madness the most humiliating, or profligacy the most scandalous must have been at work here for years".

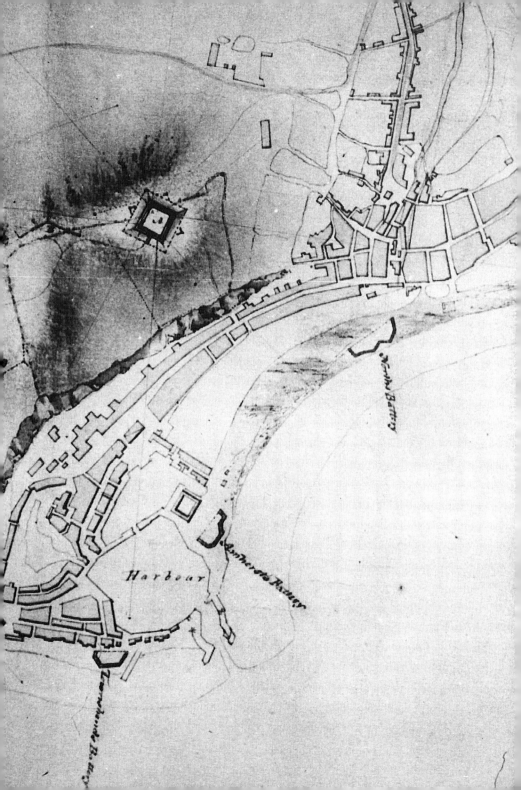

Harbour

The Grand Shaft staircase provides access between the Western Heights and the town by means of three spiral staircases which descend around a vertical, circular brick faced shaft.

The defences were only half completed when he saw them, yet he estimated that the quantity of bricks buried in the hill would have built a cottage for every labourer in Kent and Sussex. This last remark illustrated a most important aspect of the development of the fortifications in that, whereas the Norman Castle advertises its presence by being perched on a hill, the anti-Napoleonic ones are buried and are invisible from a distance, except for the unnatural angularity of the hilltop.

The plan for the fortification of the Western Heights that was drawn up by Captain William Ford in 1803, was based on the principles perfected by the famous seventeenth century French military engineer, Vauban. In outline they consisted of a Citadel on the highest ground connected by "Lines" and outlying bastions to a Redoubt overlooking the town. In addition, the Norman Castle on the other side of the valley was to be strengthened against heavy bombardment. It was also proposed (in 1814) that the fortifications on the Western Heights should be connected to the Castle by a Line cut straight across the intervening valley through the centre of the town. This would have involved the demolition of a great deal of public property and was therefore abandoned.

The first stage of construction was carried out prior to and during the French Revolutionary (1789 – 1795) and Napoleonic wars (1796 – 1815), and included the building of the Grand Shaft Barracks, the Drop Redoubt, parts of the Citadel and part of the connecting Lines. Strengthening of the Castle was also carried out at this time.

On the Western Heights construction of the Grand Shaft started in 1804 to a plan drawn up by Lieutenant-Colonel William Twiss. The Shaft provides direct access between the Heights and the town and is a most interesting form of construction. From the square of the Grand Shaft Barracks, perched on the cliffs, 59 steps descend to the bottom of a circular bowl excavated in the top of the cliff. From here three spiral staircases each of 140 steps descend around a vertical, circular brick-faced shaft, open at the top. At the bottom it is connected to Snargate Street by a horizontal tunnel emerging from the foot of the cliff. The three sets of spiral steps are lit by windows pierced in the side of the central shaft. Built to allow maximum speed of troop movement between barracks and town in case of invasion, the shaft was ready for use by 1807. When the fear of invasion passed, the Grand Shaft became a local attraction. In 1812 a Mr Leith of Walmer rode a horse up the shaft for a wager. The three staircases became segregated for three classes of society, each using a different stair, although they had to unite in the use of the steps at the top and the tunnel at the bottom.

Notices were erected to indicate who was entitled to use which set of stairs. There are various versions of these. Bavington-Jones quotes "Officers and their Ladies". "Soldiers" and "Women" respectively. Some suggest that the third staircase was designated for "Civilians". Others state that the best remembered is "Officers and their Ladies", "Sergeants and their Wives" and "Soldiers and their Women".

Ireland, in his *"History of Kent"*, published in 1829 said "such a union of elegance and convenience might have reflected credit even upon the genius of Sir Christopher Wren, at once combining the gracefulness of the stupendous vestige of architectural skill, 'the Monument of London', with the greatest simplicity and general accommodation".

Above and slightly north of the Grand Shaft, and contemporary with it, were the Grand Shaft Barracks which housed 1,200 men.

The interior of the Grand Shaft, looking upward

These, together with a military hospital that was located near to the Archcliffe Gate, were constructed in 1803. From the barracks a long flight of steps rose to the Drop Redoubt which was completed in 1808. At the extreme eastern end of the Heights, it commanded extensive views of the town, valley and harbour. From here, on the arrival of royalty, official salutes were fired and a flag was always kept flying. During the excavations for the Redoubt the foundations of a Roman Pharos were unearthed. Its twin still exists within the Castle walls on the

A magnificent view of the Drop Redoubt. At the right-hand side of the picture can be seen the Grand Shaft Barracks and the sharply defined "Line" leading to the Citadel.

other side of the valley and is acknowledged to be the oldest building in Britain. With the aid of these two lighthouses, constructed in the second century A.D. the Roman galleys were able to set course for the harbour between the two beacons.

The Citadel occupies the highest ground on the Heights, being about one hundred feet higher than the Redoubt. It was the stronghold of the fortress and fulfilled the same function as the Norman Keep at the Castle. It consisted of masked batteries, a large parade ground surrounded by store-houses and barracks, and water was supplied from a 420 foot deep well. The Lines and outlying Bastions connecting the Citadel and the Redoubt were in course of construction in 1814 when the Armistice with France was signed. After this all work on the Heights ceased and for nearly forty years the hill was riddled with a meaningless honeycomb until 1853, when because of the impending unification of Germany and the threat of Napoleon III the Royal Commission of 1859 recommended the continuation of the work.

The second stage included the completion of the North and South Lines, the formation of the ground between the Citadel and the Drop Redoubt, the construction of barracks and an officers' mess and the completion of the Western Outworks.

It was essential for the Citadel to have a direct view of the Redoubt and this involved removing the top of the hill. The excavated material was found to be useful when forming the earthworks and steep escarpments and gives the Heights a complicated angular silhouette.

Nearly four miles of Lines, which are the equivalent of mediæval moats, were constructed and linked the Redoubt to the Citadel and these in turn to the cliff face. The Lines were cut in the solid chalk and had either 18 inch brick linings or flint linings coursed in brickwork. Their height varies between 30 and 50 feet and they have a width of 30 feet. Wherever they turn an angle, deep wells prevent direct passage along the floor of the moat; these wells are overlooked by galleries running behind the moat walls from which musket fire could be directed down either of the angles formed by the moat.

A typical section of the "Lines" linking the North Centre Bastion to the Drop Redoubt in the far distance. The bridges are part of the roadway through the North Entrance

The North Centre Bastion in the North Lines

The North Centre Bastion carried out the same function as towers in the curtain wall of a mediæval castle and facilitated transverse fire along the line of the fortifications which prevented the enemy from approaching too close to the main line of defence by means of parallels and traverses. The Lines have casemates formed behind parts of their walls and at salient angles caponnières were thrust out into the ditch. The hill top is criss-crossed with these Lines which were constructed without any apparent regard to its contours; indeed at one place a Line descends 200 feet at 45 degrees, turns an acute angle at the bottom, and laboriously ascends again. The scaffolding, stagings and labour required to excavate these enormous ditches and the transportation of the spoil material must have constituted a massive engineering task.

Two of many cartoons produced at the time of the expected French invasion 1793-1814

above: 7" Rifle breech loading gun of the type intended to be mounted on the Western Heights

below: Armstrong 110lb gun circa 1860 on a sloping carriage

Included in the second stage was a requirement for additional troop accommodation and this resulted in the construction of the bomb-proof South Front Barracks in 1860. A huge trench was excavated on the slopes of the hill facing the sea and the barracks were then built along the centre of this trench.

The South Front Barracks, before demolition.   see also the illustration on page 20

The various floor levels were connected to the hill behind by a series of cast-iron bridges and galleries. The bomb-proof structure of the building took the form of a series of very thick cross walls roofed over with massive earth-covered brick barrel vaults. Just above the barracks were the Married Soldiers' Quarters which were constructed in 1859.

Within the walls of the Citadel an Officers' Mess was constructed and this took the form of a long red-brick building with stone dressings designed in a mock-Tudor country house style, with a central hall and ceremonial staircase. The Mess had a wonderful view across the Channel and was approached by steep sweeping symmetrical drives which enclosed a central staircase.

The water supplies for the whole of the Heights and Citadel were provided by steam power.

The Officers' Mess in the Citadel

The Western Outworks were constructed in order to protect the exposed western flanks of the Citadel. These works have a wedge-shaped plan and culminated at the point of the wedge in a double caponnière, flanked on either side by casemates, surrounded by two

Part of the North Lines showing one of the bridges of the North Entrance.

semi-circular ditches with the whole being designed symmetrically about a centre line. The eastern entrance to the Citadel was provided with a massive gateway complete with battered walls and is vaguely reminiscent of a pylon in an Egyptian temple.

There were two vehicular approaches to the Heights. From the south side the long winding road from the Ropewalk passed the South Front Barracks and entered the fortifications through the forbiddingly-designed Archcliffe Gate. From the north a steep hill ascended from Worthington Street and following a number of sharp turns passed over a deep moat by means of a bridge, passed over another deep moat and entered a narrow tunnel guarded by a sliding door, once more turned sharp left, then right and emerged into a deep cutting, surely an approach worthy of this impregnable fortress.

Archcliffe Gate on South Military Road (now demolished)

Enclosed within the boundaries of these fortification were two places of worship. The Church of the Knights Templar, whose foundations formed a circular chancel and a rectangular nave, was the site at which King John is reputed to have made subjection to Pandulph, the Pope's Legate, in the year 1213. On the opposite side of the road was a small military chapel with a bell turret which was built in or about 1857 in the Church Commissioners' Gothic style.

The South Front Barracks one year after the photograph on page 16 was taken (now demolished)

The bombproof Soldiers' Quarters in the Drop Redoubt

The Officers' Quarters in the Drop Redoubt, with the "Bredenstone", the remains of a Roman Pharos, above

At this time two projects were being undertaken at the Castle. A large officers' quarters was constructed within the Castle walls in 1857,. The other project under construction in this area was Fort George, which was later renamed Fort Burgoyne. The Fort itself looked north over the downs and bomb-proof casemates were built in the wings.

With the construction in 1861 of Fort Burgoyne, north of the castle the whole plan had been completed. The Western Heights and Castle could house 4,000 and 3,000 men respectively and Dover became a key centre for the British Army. During the following fifty years the town expanded and passed through its most prosperous phase. Since the resumption of work in 1853 the fortifications had cost the nation about £700,000. It is a curious twist of fate that both of the military ventures at Dover proved to be ghastly failures. When it was completed in 1909 the £4 million Admiralty Harbour was the largest artificial harbour in the world. It was abandoned by the Admiralty in 1920 owing to its vulnerability to long-range artillery.

The military fortifications which were the strongest in the country were completed in 1860 and abandoned in 1920 because the barrack accommodation was condemned. Whilst the harbour has proved useful for other purposes, the fortifications have only been used once in recent history when Admiral Ramsey fortified the Western Heights and Castle during the Second World War to counter the possibility of German invasion.

After the Second World War the Castle was returned to the Ministry of Works and in more recent times has been transferred to English Heritage. By contrast, the Western Heights Fortifications were vacated and allowed to fall into decay. In the mid-1950s there was an acute shortage of housing and some of the Grand Shaft Barracks and married quarters were renovated and put into use. However with the subsequent construction of local council houses these buildings were no longer needed and were finally demolished in the 1960s.

As a result of an acute shortage of prison accommodation in the 1950s the Citadel was selected as an ideal location for a new "House of Correction", being entirely surrounded by deep moats and already constructed. The casemates provided excellent cells and the moats which were illuminated at night, proved impassable. In 1956, the

Prison Commissioners relinquished the Citadel to HM Borstal Institution, the staff of which were housed in a newly built estate of prefabricated bungalows forming a white sub-topia to the yellow-grey fortress.

By the 1950s most of the fortifications were still structurally sound but had started to decay. Sections of the facings of the moats had collapsed, brick arches had cracked and dropped and the pointing was in poor condition. Under the guardianship of English Heritage Dover Castle has been extensively repaired and renovated, but on the infinitely grander Napoleonic fortifications on the Western Heights only limited repairs have been undertaken.

From an historical viewpoint these fortifications are as important as the Norman Castle and one day will be recognised as such. For this reason it is essential that these remarkable structures are preserved.

A mid 19th Century view showing soldiers of the Garrison looking out over the harbour.

The Military Hospital at Archcliffe (now demolished)

The Western Outworks to the Citadel (now filled in)

A section of the Grand Shaft Barracks (now demolished)

The end elevation of the officers Mess in the Citadel

25

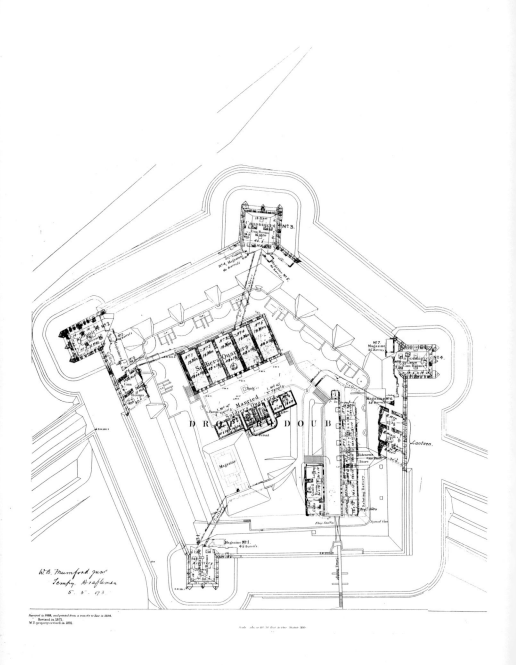

Plan of the Drop Redoubt showing the four caponniéres each linked by a tunnel to the centre of the Redoubt

26

The
FORTIFICATIONS
1959 – 1995

Their Decline
and Preservation

A Report of
JOHN PEVERLEY'S TALK
to the
DOVER SOCIETY
on 8th April 1991

The Western Outworks before they were buried
(see photo p.24)

The site of the Western Outworks at the present day

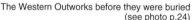

IN 1920 THE BARRACKS ON THE WESTERN HEIGHTS were classed as sub-standard and unacceptable for their purpose, but in 1950, at the time of the author's first interest in the Heights, the Army was still nominally in control although it was in the process of making a tactical withdrawal. The first significant change was in 1954 when the Citadel and Western Outworks were taken over by the Prison Commissioners who have remained in possession ever since. All credit must be given to them for investing in and maintaining the Citadel and its surrounding Lines, but in the process they have also been insensitive to its historical character by the demolitions they have perpetrated, the additions they have built and the alterations they have made.

One of their more notable acts of vandalism was in 1959 when the Western Outworks and some of the Lines around them, built in 1858, were, for no apparent reason, filled in. The Western Outworks and the Lines are buried under the fill material and could at some future date be restored.

The next great loss, reported in the *Dover Express* on 20th November 1959, was the demolition by the War Department of the grand and ingenious 1860s South Front Barracks, in the lead up to the transfer of War Department land to the Dover Corporation. In July 1961 the same newspaper, in describing the negotiations for the sale of the 126 acres of the Western Heights to the Corporation, mentioned a proposal to use the four miles of moats, or Lines, as an answer to Dover's rubbish tipping problems and that the idea was to fill the Lines, grass them over and make the area safe and attractive.

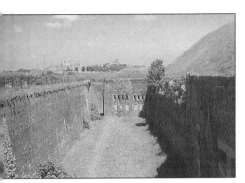

The North Links guarded by a casemate of the Drop Redoubt in the distance

A temporary bridge into the Drop Redoubt (on the right) with a caponniére beyond

John Peverley was studying in America when he heard of this idea and he immediately wrote to Kent County Council and the Ministry of Public Buildings and Works (now the Department of the Environment), objecting to the proposals to fill in the Lines.

He drew their attention to the historic importance of the Napoleonic Fortifications and suggested that the area be protected by scheduling it as an Ancient Monument.

The Ministry, obviously feeling the pangs of conscience asked for copies of his photographs and about a year later, in August 1962, the Western Heights were given this very necessary protection. The Town Council's concern at this move was evident when an article in the *Dover Express* quoted the Town Clerk, Mr James A. Johnson, as saying "it is a piece of nonsense:".

In an article in the same newspaper in November 1963 it was noted that the Council's minutes stated that "the negotiations between Dover Corporation and the War Department were nearly complete but that they had been greatly extended by the intervention of the Ministry of Public Buildings and Works in scheduling the Western Heights as an Ancient Monument".

The 1963 article also referred to the wish of the Dover Corporation to demolish the North Entrance (built about 1857) and to build a new approach road to open the Heights for development. The peculiar design of the Entrance being considered to be a very special part of the fortifications, the Ministry would not agree to its demolition. It did, however, agree with the Corporation's proposal to build a new bridge

Archcliffe Gate, demolished at the time of the formation of the present day viewing point (right above)

to span the North Lines. Reference was also made to the expense of building the new road and bridge and that as a result the cost of purchasing the Heights had been reduced by £2,000 to £20,250! Mr James A. Johnson, the Town Clerk, was quoted as saying "except for the use of the moats for refuse disposal, the settlement now put forward was approximately similar to that which the Corporation had wanted before the Ministry had intervened".   .

In the 1960s, possibly connected with the transfer of land to the Corporation, Archcliffe Gate was demolished and the first part of the Line running thence to the Ropewalk was filled in. The road at that point was widened and a car park and viewing point were constructed. The Garrison Chapel was demolished and the land used for housing the Prison Officers' families. The Military Hospital, on land behind the present day P&O head-quarters was also demolished and an engineering works subsequently built in its place.

In February 1965 the parallel ranges of the Grand Shaft Barracks were demolished and during their demolition the area was used as one of the locations for the BBC film "War Games" depicting life in Britain after a nuclear bomb attack.

During 1966 it was reported that the purchase of the Western Heights by Dover Corporation had not ben completed and that this was due to the long drawn out wrangling over the cost of the new approach road and to the decision of the Ministry to extend the area it wished to take into its guardianship. In the same year the Dover corporation sealed the Grand Shaft staircases on the grounds of public safety. There was

The Inner Doors of the Original North Entrance   The new road cutting through the "Line"

great concern that this might be the first step towards demolition or filling in and there was a flurry of correspondence between the New Dover Group (predecessor of the Dover Society) and the local MP, David Ennals, stressing the need for the preservation of the staircase.

In 1967, work on the new approach road across the North Lines suddenly commenced and was speedily completed. Regrettably it did not span the moats as originally agreed between the Corporation and the Ministry, but cut through them at a much lower level with a sweeping curve and wide embankments and as a result the integrity of the Western Heights as an impregnable fortress was completely lost. Twenty-five years later the only people benefiting from the construction of the road are those associated with the Youth Custody Institution.

In 1978 the Home Office Prison Department blatantly bulldozed a Napoleonic Magazine in the Citadel in order to build a boiler house and chimney, which disfigured the skyline. They did this without consulting the Department of the Environment or the Dover District Council which they were obliged to do under the Ancient Monuments legislation. This created a public outcry and a protracted debate on the matter. Successful protests were made to the Ombudsman by the New Dover Group for the lack of consultation and the Department of the Environment for doing nothing about it. The Home Office's explanation was described as unsatisfactory and inconsistent with other sources. The Ombudsman concluded his comments by saying "I find its (the Home Office's) performance in the whole unhappy business deplorable and disturbing ...I can only hope that both the DoE and the Home Office have learned important lessons and that there will be no further incidents of this kind".[1]

Early in 1990, after English Heritage had assumed responsibility for the Western Heights, the Home Office constructed an accommodation block at the Young Offenders Institution (the former Borstal) without consulting either English Heritage or the Department of the Environment, although this time it did inform Dover District Council.

The Council confined its comments to the appearance of the roof and the brickwork, apparently unaware of the further threats to the White Cliffs skyline which had become even more important to Dover's tourist image because of the threat of the Channel Tunnel to local employment. The Dover Society protested to the Ombudsman that once again the Home Office had flouted the Ancient Monument legislation as it affected the Western Heights. The Ombudsman strongly criticised the Home Office for failing to learn the lessons of the 1981 report and for repeating its mistake. The Permanent Secretary apologised and said that new instructions had been sent to staff and oral guidance given to senior staff on procedures for dealing with Ancient Monuments. He concluded with the hope that this time measures had been taken unfailingly to prevent any recurrence.

The Western Heights cover a large area and considerable sections of the fortifications have received no attention for many years and are quietly becoming submerged as nature takes over. This may provide a form of protection, providing the basic structure remains sound, but it is difficult to be sure of this. Externally the pentagonal fortress, the Drop Redoubt, appears to be in good condition. It is in the care of English Heritage who admit they currently do not have the resources to bring the Redoubt into a condition that is satisfactory for safe public access.

The North Centre Bastion is now very overgrown and a similar situation exists in the South Lines to the west of the Citadel and along most of the North Lines. Something akin to a nature reserve is being created but this is hardly in character with the fortress. On the other hand the North Outworks have been kept clear and in reasonable condition.

In conclusion, it is interesting to see how as a result of joint funding from District Councils, County Councils, English Heritage and private Trusts, other Napoleonic forts around Portsmouth and Chatham have

---

[1] The chimney was demolished in 1995 when the heating system changed from solid fuel to gas

been satisfactorily restored and opened to the public. The fortification of the Western Heights are acknowledged as outstanding in their own right and it is hoped that the District and County Councils and English Heritage would agree that they merit extensive restoration work as soon as adequate funding is available. It is, however, possible that they will always be destined to suffer from being too close to one of English Heritage's main tourist attractions, Dover Castle.

Philomena Kennedy's drawing showing some of the orchids to be found on the Western Heights

The
WESTERN HEIGHTS
1989 – 1995

A Special Place

KIRK ALEXANDER
Project Manager
White Cliffs Countryside Project

THE FORTIFICATIONS OF THE WESTERN HEIGHTS are a Scheduled Ancient Monument, largely owned by English Heritage, except for the Citadel, which the Home Office runs as a Young Offenders Institution. Dover District Council owns most of the green slopes, which act as a "green lung" to Dover, bringing the countryside close to the centre of town. Indeed, wild orchids can be found growing less than three hundred metres from the Market Square. In 1994 the Dover District Council declared a Local Nature Reserve to help protect the Heights in the future.

Enter the White Cliffs Countryside Project

The White Cliffs Countryside Project was launched in December 1989, with the aim of helping landowners care for the internationally famous cliffs and countryside around Dover and Folkestone, as part of a strategy to attract more tourists and new employment to the area. The Western Heights were an early priority for action. The Project is a unique collaboration between the local authorities (Dover District Council, Shepway District Council, Kent County Council), conservation organisations (Kent Trust for Nature Conservation, Countryside Commission, English Nature) and the private sector (Eurotunnel), now joined by English Heritage and British Rail. Such a partnership is very cost effective; every £1 contributed by Dover District Council is matched by more than £6 from other sources.

Ancient Chalk Grassland

The Green Slopes, designated a Site of Nature Conservation Interest by the Kent Trust for Nature Conservation, are ancient chalk grasslands, which when well-managed can contain 30-40 plant species in a single square yard, including many plants rarely found in more recent

grassland. David Bellamy, in his visit to Dover in 1994, described these chalk grasslands as the "European equivalent of tropical rain forests", as they are one of the richest plant habitats in Europe.

Chalk Grassland needs to be Grazed

The slopes of the Western Heights were grazed until the 1950's, but since then the chalk grassland has been slowly invaded by shrubs and trees, shading out the rare wild flowers. Aerial photographs show how much has been lost in the last thirty years. In the spring of 1990 grazing was reintroduced to the fourteen acres of chalk grassland around the Drop Redoubt, and to a further six acres at St Martin's Battery in 1991.

In the winter 1991/92 the unsafe and unsightly fencing around the Drop Redoubt were replaced with financial assistance from English Heritage. In the spring of 1992, grazing was extended to the 59 acres behind Clarendon and Maxton, following consultation with local people. It was agreed that grazing would be organised on a rotation, with some areas free of grazing at any one time to allow people to let their dogs run free. Finally, in 1993 grazing started on the 47 acres of chalk grassland behind Aycliffe.

All of these areas have been accepted into the Countryside Steward-ship scheme, operated by the Countryside Commission, which provides grant aid to help re-establish traditional management of landscapes such as the chalk downlands.

The Dexter Cattle

We were fortunate to be offered by a local farmer Dexter cattle to graze on the Western Heights. The cattle originate from the mountains

 of Western Ireland and they thrive on poor quality grazing. They are the smallest breed of cattle in Britain, and with their lightweight and short legs can graze the steep slopes without damaging the precious turf. In addition, many have been hand reared so are friendly to people. They are also virtually silent so will not keep the neighbours awake.

Explore the Western Heights

The White Cliffs Countryside Project with the help of local volunteers has improved footpaths by building steps on steep slopes and waymarking the main routes. One of the first tasks was the restoration of Cowgate Steps, an important part of the ancient monument, using traditional materials to create an attractive "grand entrance" for visitors. English Heritage has allowed access into the moats around the Drop

Redoubt, and the Home Office has agreed in principle to allow permissive access to the open space around the Citadel Battery.

By encouraging more people to walk the Western Heights, there has been a marked reduction in flytipping and vandalism: anti-social activities do not usually continue in front of an audience. Local people have helped as voluntary wardens, and their watchful eye has largely cured flytipping along the North Military Road.

Understanding the Western Heights

A further aim is to explain the historical and wildlife attractions of the Western Heights. Information boards were installed at entrances and a colour leaflet was produced with financial assistance from Dover District Council. Dover Museum installed a history trail around the Drop Redoubt and Grand Shaft areas. The White Cliffs Countryside Project started an active programme of guided walks, with innovative walks involving landscape and wild flower photography. 1994 saw the start of storytelling and theatrical walks to try to bring to life for everybody the history of the Western Heights.

Thanks to all the Volunteers

There are many ways for people of all ages to get involved. The White Cliffs Countryside Volunteers, joined by local community groups such as Astor School, Dover College, Dover Grammar School for Girls and the Girls' Venture Corps have helped clear footpaths and install hundreds of steps. A retired miner has single-handedly transformed the footpaths behind Clarendon. The Royal Green Jackets abseiled walls to clear the accumulated rubbish from the moats. Scrub has been cleared, especially from within the moats whose walls might be damaged by the growing trees. It should be emphasised that there is no intention to remove all scrub and tree, as they are great value for nesting and migrating birds.

Local people help protect the Heights as voluntary wardens, keeping a watchful eye, and they have been successful in reducing vandalism and flytipping. Local volunteers have helped lead guided walks.

Schools have been using the Heights as an outdoor classroom, where they learn a wide range of skills contained in the National Curriculum. Education packs for primary and secondary schools have been produced with generous sponsorship from Eurotunnel.

Enter Europe

In 1994 the White Cliffs Countryside Project was successful in obtaining grant aid from the Transfrontier Programme of the European Regional Development Fund.

Floodlighting was installed around the Drop Redoubt, to match the floodlighting of Dover Castle on the opposite side of the valley. A programme of environmental improvements is planned for the Grand Shaft and St Martin's Battery areas. An interpretation trail, known as the Soldiers Life, around the Grand Shaft Barracks area, is intended to complement the enhanced Grand Shaft entrance in Snargate Street. In addition, an interpretation trail will be laid out around St Martin's Battery, as the first stage of creating a Discovery Centre here for the whole of the Western Heights.

You can Help : *Much remains to be done.*

Anyone wishing to help should contact the White Cliffs Countryside Project at 6 Cambridge Terrace, Dover, Kent CT16 1JT.
Telephone: 01304 241806